All rights reserved. No part of this publication may be reproduced, distributed, or transmitted in any form or by any means, including photocopying, recording or other electronic or mechanical methods, without the prior written permission of the publisher, except in the case of brief quotations embodied in reviews and certain other non-commercial uses permitted by copyright law.

Copyright © 2016 by Forrest Willett

ISBN-13: 978-1523728367
Images by: A. Kumar
Back photo by: Natalie Alexia
Formatting by: Lise Cartwright

www.Loveisthetrueblack.com

To have Forrest speak at your school, go to www.forrestwillett.com

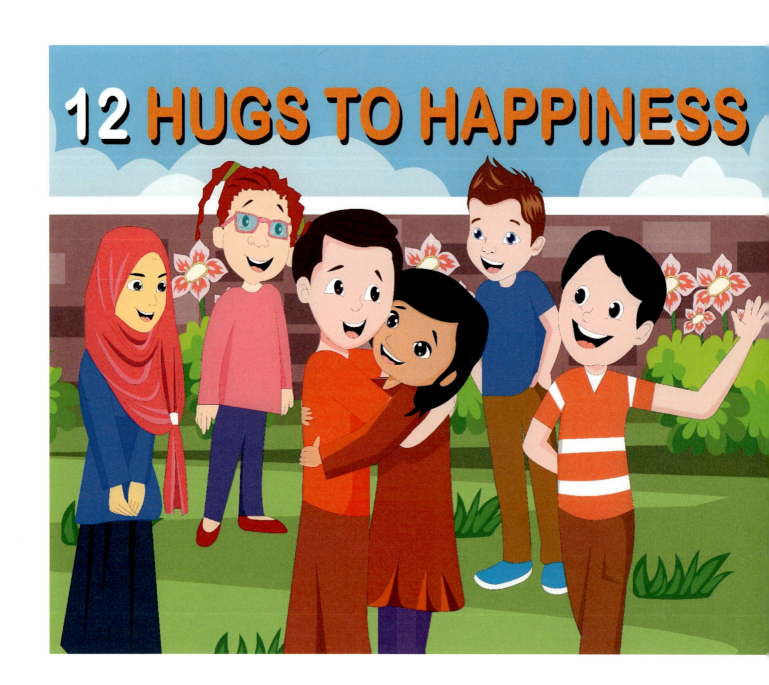

This book is dedicated to my wife, Julie and my son, Hunter, who make sure I get 12 hugs every day!

To Patty Aubery and Jack Canfield, who introduced me to the concept of '12 hugs to happiness,' which has forever changed my life.

"May you always stay humble and kind"

Dear Noah,
Love from Auntie Stphie
xox
Hugs!!

This Book Belongs To:

_____

Everyday, Forrest carried what he thought were his only friends to school in his backpack. Their names were Sad and Lonely.

They were very heavy friends, so Forrest walked really slow and hunched over. The weight of them also pulled down Forrest's face, which made it hard for him to smile.

One day, while Forrest sat in the corner of the playground with Sad and Lonely, Phil and Buti, two boys from Forrest's classroom, asked Forrest if he wanted to play?

Forrest replied, "No." So the boys went off to play and have fun with the other children in the playground.

As Forrest watched the other kids play and have fun, he could not help but think to himself that he also wanted to play and have fun.

"Why did I say no when they asked me to play?" Forrest asked himself.

As Forrest pulled his lunch out of his backpack, he saw his two old friends, Sad and Lonely, and in the bottom, he also saw a very small and unfamiliar guest.

Forrest reached down and lifted his new friend out of the backpack. She was extremely heavy.

Although she was smaller than Sad and Lonely, she weighed more than both of them together.

"What's your name?" Forrest asked the little one.

"I'm, I'm, I'm Anxious" she replied with a trembling voice.

"I don't feel well, can I just go back in the backpack now? That's my comfort zone and I feel safe in there, it makes me nervous to be around others."

Right then the bell rang and Forrest hurried to put all three back in his backpack where they could all be comfortable.

On the way back to the school, Forrest really noticed the weight of his backpack.

Forrest struggled with all of this strength to go back in the school and finish the day.

After school, Forrest went right home and crawled into bed, he was so tired!

Forrest's older sister, Jesse said; "supper is ready."

Forrest was tired from carrying all that weight. He did not feel like eating. He just wanted to sleep.

So Jesse shut the light off and let Forrest sleep all night.

The next morning, Jesse shook Forrest to wake him. Forrest looked very, very tired and asked Jesse if he could sleep some more.

Jesse replied, "You know the rules. If you are going to live with me, you have to do your chores and go to school everyday."

"I know," Forrest replied, "but just this one time, can I sleep in?"

"OK" Jesse replied, feeling sorry for Forrest. "But only until lunchtime, then I will drive you to school. Your teacher, Ms. Aubery, said there is a special guest coming to school this afternoon and you don't want to miss out."

After lunch, Jesse drove Forrest to school. He was feeling refreshed with a lot more energy, as he did not have to carry the weight of his backpack to school that day.

Just as Jesse brought Forrest into the school, Ms. Aubery held Forrest by the hand and said, "Let's hurry; our special guest is going to speak to the school and I don't want you to miss it."

Jesse waived goodbye with a smile as Ms. Aubery led Forrest to the gymnasium where the special guest was about to start talking.

As the large doors opened, Forrest froze with fear and started to sweat.

"What's wrong Forrest?" asked Ms. Aubery.

"I don't feel so good," said Forrest.

All of the eyes of the children were on Forrest and Ms. Aubery as the large doors slammed shut behind them.

Forrest said, "I will just stand back here, by the doors."

Ms. Aubery took Forrest's hand and said with a smile, "Look, there are two spots up front. You can sit with me."

Mr. Wittal, the school's principal, introduced today's special guest, Mr. Canfield.

All of the children clapped with excitement!

Mr. Canfield had some really funny slides with cartoons that made everyone laugh. Even Forrest.

Mr. Canfield explained the importance of laughter to the children.

He said that laughter gives you a sense of wellbeing. It is nature's way of making you feel good, even if you are in pain.

Forrest looked at Phil sitting next to him, who had a broken arm from playing rugby, and even Phil was laughing.

"Doesn't your arm hurt from laughing so hard Phil?" asked Forrest.

"Not at all," Phil replied, with a big grin!

Over the afternoon, all of the children participated in several sharing exercises.

One of them was to share one thing you are grateful for.

Kathleen shared with Forrest she was grateful for her new bike. Abdul shared with Liz he was grateful for her friendship. Jan shared with Jaime she was grateful for her new dog.

Now ask yourself this: What are you grateful for?

After a short break, something happened that would change Forrest's life forever.

From the stage, Mr. Canfield asked for a volunteer, but no hands were raised.

Ms. Aubery raised Forrest's hand up high in the air and said, "Over here!!"

Once again, Forrest froze and his face went red, as all eyes were on him.

"Well, come on up here son." Mr. Canfield said with a smile.

As Forrest climbed up the stairs, each one felt like a mountain.

Mr. Canfield read off a slide that said, "Each day you need: 4 hugs for survival, 8 hugs for maintenance, 12 hugs for growth.

Mr. Canfield then asked, by a show of hands, "How many of you have received 12 hugs today?"

No hands were raised.

Mr. Canfield looked at Forrest and asked, "What's your name, son?"

"Forrest" he replied nervously. "That is a nice name. I am grateful to meet you, Forrest! Now Forrest, do you know how to give a proper hug?"

"No," Forrest replied. "No? Why not?" asked Mr. Canfield with a huge smile.

"Because no one hugs me," replied Forrest. Mr. Canfield's eyes went big and glossy as he said, "Well Forrest today is the day all of that will change!"

"To give a proper hug, you will have to take that backpack off. Let me help you!"

"Boy, that's a heavy backpack Forrest. What have you got in there?" asked Mr. Canfield.

"Those are my friends. I take them everywhere. Their names are Sad, Lonely and Anxious."

Mr. Canfield said, "Today you will go home with some new friends that won't weigh you down. They will lift you up! Now, before we get started, lets unpack these unneeded travelers and get rid of them."

Mr. Canfield found a new home for Sad, Lonely and Anxious in the trashcan on the side of the stage.

Forrest looked excited, his face exploded with a great big smile.

"Now Forrest, the proper way to give a hug is your left ear will touch my left ear, that also places your heart on my heart."

"And you may want to hug for about 20 seconds, without saying a word. Just be present for the other person," said Mr. Canfield.

This was very strange, and a good feeling at the same time for Forrest. As he had not experienced many hugs before, not even from his parents.

There was always a lot of yelling and screaming at Forrest's house, and for that reason, Forrest's mom moved far away, and Forrest went to live with his older sister, Jesse.

Mr. Canfield said to the students, "Now that you all know how to give a proper hug, let's stand up and get some hugs."

After a few minutes passed, Mr. Canfield asked the students to take a look around the room. "Now what do you see on everyone's faces?" he asked.

Everyone replied, "SMILES!"

"That's right," said Mr. Canfield, "So remember whatever it is you want in life, give it! If you want more hugs, give more hugs. If you want more friends, go out and be a friend."

Forrest started to count the number of hugs he gave and received…

Jamie 1, Mayra 2, Antonio 3, Lise 4, Jan 5, Bob 6, Shawn 7, Ricky 8, Alice 9, Joss 10, Michael 11, Miriam 12, Rosana 13, Donna 14, Noah 15, Ms. Aubery 16… Even Kenny O'Conner, the schools star basketball player, gave Forrest a hug: 17.

"Wow, 17 hugs in one day!" said Forrest. Forrest had never felt so much love and happiness in his life.

Mr. Canfield shared with the group, "That you can create this feeling of love and happiness anywhere in the world, and that happiness does not come from having more toys than the next person."

"Happiness comes from inside you, from giving and receiving love."

Mr. Canfield called Forrest back on stage, where he thanked him for volunteering and presented Forrest with two balloons.

"Hugs and Happiness." Mr. Canfield tied them to Forrest's backpack and said, "Take these new friends everywhere you go and you will never feel Sad, Lonely or Anxious again."

From that day forward, Forrest felt a lift in his spirits and now walked with a spring in his step and a smile on his face.

Forrest also makes sure a day does not go by without giving and receiving 12 hugs to happiness.

Everyone thanked Forrest for sharing how he felt, and they now know it is ok to share how they feel with others. Shawn and Ricky said they will be friends for life!

Inga shared how she felt anxious when she auditioned for the school play.

Amina shared how she felt lonely when she first moved here from India.

Russ shared how he felt sad for a long time after he lost his grandmother.

The children realized that once they shared their feelings with each other, they felt much better.

Now let's see if you can give and receive 12 hugs to your happiness everyday!

Visit www.forrestwillett.com to have Forrest speak at your school.

Manufactured by Amazon.ca
Bolton, ON